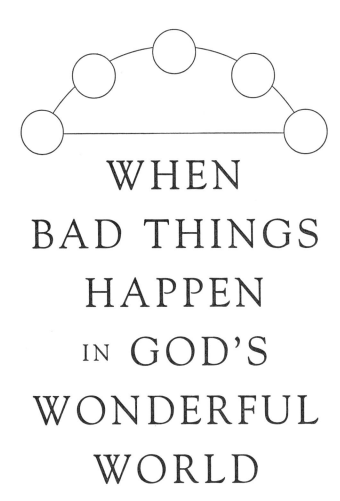

# WHEN
# BAD THINGS
# HAPPEN
## IN GOD'S
# WONDERFUL
# WORLD

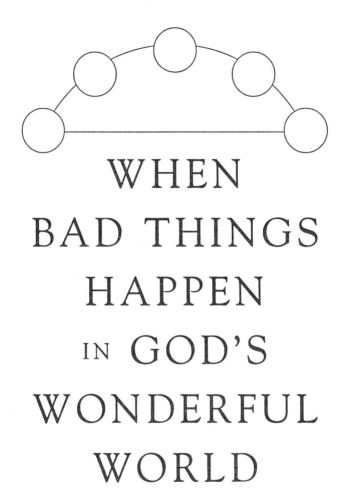

# WHEN BAD THINGS HAPPEN IN GOD'S WONDERFUL WORLD

*A Book for Children and Their Parents*

*The quoted ideas expressed in this book (but not scripture verses) are not, in all cases, exact quotations, as some have been edited for clarity and brevity. In all cases, the author has attempted to maintain the speaker's original intent. In some cases, quoted material for this book was obtained from secondary sources, primarily print media. While every effort was made to ensure the accuracy of these sources, the accuracy cannot be guaranteed. For additions, deletions, corrections or clarifications in future editions of this text, please write* ELM HILL BOOKS.
P. O. BOX 141000
NASHVILLE, TN 37214

Scripture quotations are taken from:

New Century Version © 1987, 1988, 1991 by W. Publishing, a division of Thomas Nelson, Inc. All rights reserved. Used by permission.

International Children's Bible®, New Century Version® Copyright © 1986, 1988, 1999 by Tommy Nelson®, a division of Thomas Nelson, Inc. Nashville, TN 37214. Used by permission.

Cover Design by Karen Phillips
Page Layout by Bart Dawson

ISBN 1-4041-8458-9

*Printed in the United States of America*

# TABLE OF CONTENTS

# A MESSAGE TO PARENTS

**B**ecause you're a concerned parent or grandparent, you know that your child is full of questions about the hopes and heartbreaks that sometimes accompany life in our troubled world. During these challenging times, many of your child's questions will result from the unending stream of media images that bombard your family at every turn. Despite your best efforts to protect your youngster, he or she will encounter the harsh realities of good and evil. This text is intended to help you, as a loving parent, discuss these issues with your son or daughter.

As you read these pages with your child, it is important that you take ample time to share *your own* feelings about God's role in our world. Whether you realize it or not, *you* are your child's most important role model. And even though you certainly can't provide all of the answers, you *can* help your child grapple with the important questions that he or she is sure to ask.

In using this book, here are a few tips:

1. Read this book *with* your children, and take time to explain the meanings of its essays, quotations, and Bible verses.

2. As you read, ask your child lots of open-ended questions: this book is intended to open a dialogue between you and your child, but if all your questions can be answered with "yes" or "no," that dialogue will soon become a monologue.

3. If you find that a chapter is particularly helpful for your child, revisit it frequently.

God has created a wonderful world, and He offers each of us the gift of life—both abundant and eternal. But God's world is not free from evil nor is it free from pain. As parents, we must help our children understand that when bad things happen in God's wonderful world He stands ready, willing, and perfectly able to repair the damage. Our job, of course, is to let Him.

# IN THE BEGINNING

God made the world and every-thing in it. And when God was finished, He saw that His creation was *very* good indeed. God made the heavens and the earth, and He made people like you and me. When God made us, He gave us the power to make choices for our-selves. From the earliest days, we human beings have, at times, made choices that were not very smart. Just ask Adam and Eve.

Adam and Eve were the first man and woman. God gave them every-thing they needed to live happily-ever-after in a lovely place called the Garden of Eden. But God warned them *not* to eat the fruit of a particular tree. So what do you think Adam and Eve did? They disobeyed God and ate the fruit anyway! It was a *very* big mistake that led to lots of trouble.

Like Adam and Eve, God has given each of us the ability to make our own decisions about the way that we behave. Unfortunately, some people choose to behave badly, and when they do, these people cause bad things to happen in God's beautiful world (just like Adam and Eve invited trouble into the Garden of Eden).

This book will help you understand what the Bible says about the good things and the bad things that happen in this world. And, when bad things *do* happen—as they most certainly will—please remember that God is always good (even when some people aren't). And please remember that God always has the last word. Always!

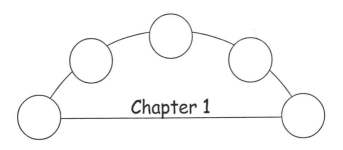

Chapter 1

# WHEN BAD THINGS HAPPEN IN GOD'S WONDERFUL WORLD

God is our protection and
our strength. He always helps
in times of trouble.
—

Psalm 46:1 NCV

If God is good, and if He made the world, why do bad things happen? Part of that question is easy to answer, and part of it isn't. Let's get to the easy part first: Sometimes, bad things happen because people choose to disobey God's rules.

When people break the rules—especially *God's* rules—they invite sadness and trouble into our beautiful world; it's unfortunate but it happens. That's why brave folks like police officers and soldiers are sometimes needed to protect us.

But on other occasions, bad things happen, and it's *nobody's* fault. So who is to blame then? Sometimes, nobody is to blame. Sometimes, things just happen and we simply cannot know why.

Thankfully, all our questions will be answered . . . some day.

The good news is this: the Bible promises that when we finally get to heaven, we *will* understand all the reasons behind God's plans. But until then, we must simply trust Him.

So why does a perfect God allow bad things to occur? Sometimes, it's because of the bad choices that people make. And sometimes, it's because of a grand plan that we cannot see. In either case, we must trust that God is good, and that, in the end, He will make things right.

# Words to the Wise

Trust the past to God's mercy,
the present to God's love,
and the future to God's plan.
St. Augustine

Two words will help you
when you run low on hope:
accept and trust.
Charles Swindoll

God is God.
He knows what he is doing.
Max Lucado

NO MATTER WHAT

WE HAPPEN TO FACE,

CHRIST NEVER

LEAVES US.

Billy Graham

Although the world is full of hardship, it is also full of overcoming it.

Helen Keller

Measure the size of the obstacles against the size of God.

Beth Moore

Since we can't understand everything that God *does*, we must trust everything that God *is*.

Marie T. Freeman

## God's Word

Now we see as if we are looking
into a dark mirror. But at that
time, in the future, we shall see
clearly. Now I know only a part.
But at that time I will know fully,
as God has known me.

1 Corinthians 13:12 ICB

## A Prayer

Dear Lord, when things happen
that I don't fully understand,
help me put my trust in You.
Because I know that this world is
in Your hands, I am comforted.
And because I know that you love
me, I will do my best to put my
worries aside, not just for today,
but every day that I live.
—Amen—

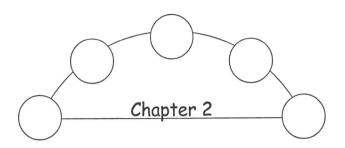

Chapter 2

# WHEN
# WE'RE AFRAID

Don't be afraid, because
the Lord your God will be with
you everywhere you go.
—

Joshua 1:9 NCV

When bad things happen, it's understandable that we might feel afraid. In fact, it's *good* to be afraid if our fears keep us from behaving foolishly (by the way, if that little voice inside your head tells you that doing something is dangerous, *don't do it*).

When our own troubles—or the world's troubles—leave us fearful, we should discuss our concerns with the people who love and care for us. Parents and grandparents can help us understand our fears, and they can help us feel better. That's why we need to talk with them.

We should also discuss our worries with our Heavenly Father. God is always ready to hear our prayers, and He can give us comfort when we feel afraid. Whenever we're uncertain about what lies ahead, we can share our concerns with God . . . and we should.

It's okay to be afraid—all of us are fearful from time to time. And it's good to know that we can talk about our fears with loved ones *and* with God. When we do, we'll discover that fear lasts for a little while, but love lasts forever.

GOD ALONE
CAN GIVE US SONGS
IN THE NIGHT.

C. H. Spurgeon

# Words to the Wise

Let nothing disturb you, nothing
frighten you; all things are
passing; God never changes.
Teresa of Avila

Fill your mind with thoughts of
God rather than thoughts of fear.
Norman Vincent Peale

In God's faithfulness lies
eternal security.
Corrie ten Boom

GOD IS, MUST BE,
THE ANSWER
TO OUR QUESTIONS
AND OUR FEARS.

Hannah Whitall Smith

# God's Word

All you who put your hope in
the Lord be strong and brave.

Psalms 31:24 NCV

# A Prayer

Dear Lord, when I am afraid,
there are people I can turn to.
I thank You, Lord, for the love
and support of my family and
friends. Help us always to share
our concerns with each other,
and help us always to take
our concerns to You in prayer.
—Amen—

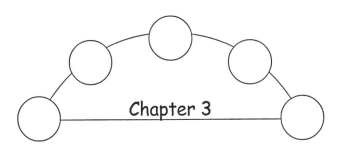

Chapter 3

# WHEN PEOPLE ARGUE AND FIGHT

People with quick tempers cause trouble, but those who control their tempers stop a quarrel.

—

Proverbs 15:18 NCV

Since the days of Cain and Abel, people have discovered plenty of things to fight about (Cain and Abel, by the way, were the sons of Adam and Eve). It seems that fighting is a favorite activity for many people, even though it's almost always the wrong thing to do.

Kids should do their best to avoid fights, period! But sometimes, adults are forced to take strong actions in order to protect our homes, our neighborhoods, and our world. It's takes lots of brave people to make our world safe and free; we should thank the men and women who help us and protect us.

On two different occasions, Jesus took quick action when He discovered moneychangers and merchants in the Temple (Matthew 21:12; John 2:12-13). These people were disobeying God's law by conducting business in a house of worship. Jesus followed His conscience and responded without delay: He physically removed the moneychangers and merchants from the Temple.

Sometimes, when grownups see bad things happening, they must respond as Jesus did: forcefully. But that doesn't mean that the Bible tells the rest of us to fight and argue. Far from it. We kids should run—not walk—away from fights and arguments. Grownups, on the other hand, must sometimes stand up for what they know to be right. And it's a good thing that they do!

## Words to the Wise

Anger is the noise of the soul.
Max Lucado

Bitterness and anger, usually over small things, cause trouble in our homes, in our churches, and in our friendships.
Warren Wiersbe

BROTHERLY LOVE IS STILL THE DISTINGUISHING MARK OF EVERY TRUE CHRISTIAN.

Matthew Henry

WE CAN ALWAYS GAUGE WHERE WE ARE BY THE TEACHINGS OF JESUS CHRIST.

Oswald Chambers

## God's Word

A foolish person enjoys doing wrong, but a person with understanding enjoys doing what is wise.

Proverbs 10:23 NCV

# A Prayer

Dear Lord, help me to turn away
from angry thoughts and angry
people. Help me always to use
Jesus as my guide for life,
and let me trust His promises
today and forever.
—Amen—

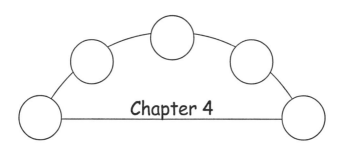

Chapter 4

# A TIME TO WALK AWAY,
# A TIME TO STAND UP
# AND BE COUNTED

I always try to do what I believe
is right before God and people.
—

Acts 24:16 NCV

When your friends misbehave, do you tell them to stop, or do you go along with the crowd? Usually, it's much easier to go along with the crowd— or to say nothing at all—but that's the wrong thing to do. It's better to stand up for what you know is right.

Sometimes, grownups must stand up for the things they believe in. When they do, it can be hard for them, too. But the Bible tells us over and over again that we should do the *right* thing, not the *easy* thing.

God's world is a wonderful place, but people who misbehave can spoil things in a hurry. So if your friends behave poorly, don't copy them! Instead, do the right thing. You'll be glad you did . . . and so will God!

TO GO AGAINST ONE'S

# CONSCIENCE

IS NEITHER SAFE NOR

RIGHT. HERE I STAND.

I CANNOT DO OTHERWISE.

Martin Luther

# Words to the Wise

Obedience to God is the outward expression of your love of God.
Henry Blackaby

Begin today to be what you will become tomorrow.
St. Jerome

Do you want to be wise?
Choose wise friends.
Charles Swindoll

# God's Word

Keep your eyes focused on what
is right, and look straight ahead
to what is good.

Proverbs 4:25 NCV

# A Prayer

Dear Lord, give me the wisdom to know right from wrong, and give me the courage to do the things that I know to be right.
—Amen—

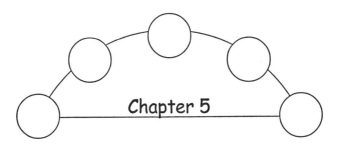

# Chapter 5

# THINGS
# THAT WE DON'T
# UNDERSTAND

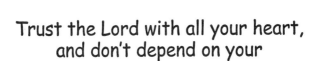

Trust the Lord with all your heart,
and don't depend on your
own understanding.

—

Proverbs 3:5 NCV

Sometimes, things happen that we simply don't understand. And that's exactly how God intends it! You see God has given us many gifts, but He *hasn't* given us the power to understand everything that happens in our world (that comes later, when we get to heaven!).

The Bible tells us God's plans are far bigger than we humans can possibly understand. That's one of the reasons that God doesn't make His plans clear to us. But even when we can't understand *why* God allows certain things to happen, we *can* trust His love for us.

The Bible does make one part of God's plan perfectly clear: we should accept His Son Jesus into our hearts so that we might have eternal life (John 3:16). And when we do, we are protected today, tomorrow, and forever.

GOD WILL DO HIS PART.

OUR PART IS

TO TRUST HIM.

A. W. Tozer

# Words to the Wise

Fear lurks in the shadows of life.
Jesus says, "Stop being afraid.
Trust me!"

Charles Swindoll

As God's children, we are
the recipients of His love—a love
that allows us to keep trusting
even when we have no idea
what God is doing.

Beth Moore

# God's Word

Whoever listens to what is taught
will succeed, and whoever trusts
the Lord will be happy.

Proverbs 16:20 NCV

# A Prayer

Dear Lord, even when I don't understand *why* things happen, I will trust You. Even when I am confused or worried, I will trust You. There are many things that I cannot do, Lord, and there are many things that I cannot understand. But one thing I *can* do is to trust You always. And I will.

—Amen—

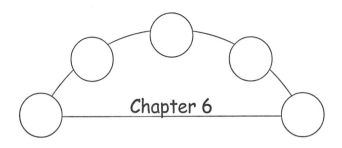

Chapter 6

# WHERE SHOULD WE TAKE OUR WORRIES?

Give your worries to the Lord, and he will take care of you. He will never let good people down.

Psalm 55:22 NCV

When we're worried, there are two places we should take our concerns: to the people who love and care for us *and* to God.

When troubles arise, it helps to talk about them with parents, grandparents, and concerned adults. But we shouldn't stop there: we should also talk to God through our prayers.

If you're worried about something, you can pray about it any time you want. And remember that God is always listening, and He always wants to hear from you.

So when you're worried, try this plan: talk and pray. Talk to the grownups who love you, and pray to the Heavenly Father who made you. The more you talk and the more you pray, the better you'll feel.

A HOME IS A PLACE
WHERE WE FIND
COMFORT
AND DIRECTION.

Gigi Graham Tchividjian

ANY CONCERN THAT IS TOO SMALL TO BE TURNED INTO A PRAYER IS TOO SMALL TO WORRY ABOUT.

Corrie ten Boom

## Words to the Wise

God is bigger than your problems.
Whatever worries press upon you
today, put them in God's hands
and leave them there.
Billy Graham

Give each day to God,
knowing that He is God over
all your tomorrows.
Kay Arthur

PRAY,

AND LET GOD WORRY.

Martin Luther

# God's Word

Jesus said, "Don't let your hearts
be troubled. Trust in God,
and trust in me."

John 14:1 NCV

# A Prayer

Dear Lord, when I am worried,
I know where to turn for help:
to those who love me, and to You.
Thank You, for the people who
love and care for me, and thank
you, Lord, for Your love. Because
of that love, I have hope and
assurance for this day
and every day.
—Amen—

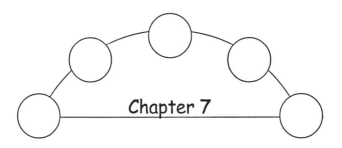

# IS IT OKAY
# TO LAUGH?

**A happy heart is like
good medicine.
—**

Proverbs 17:22 NCV

Even when times are tough, it's okay to laugh. In fact, the tougher the times, the more we may need to laugh (but the less we may feel like doing it).

Sometimes, we may feel guilty about having fun when some people around the world are not having any fun at all. But God doesn't want us to spend our lives moping around with frowns on our faces. Far from it! God tells us that a happy heart is a very good thing to have.

So if you're afraid to laugh out loud, don't be. Remember that God wouldn't have given you the gift of laughter if He hadn't intended for you to use it. And remember: if you're laughing, that *does not* mean that you're unconcerned about people who may be hurting. It simply means that you've taken a little time to have fun, and that's good because God wants you to have an abundant life and a cheerful heart.

Proverbs 17:22 says that laughter is good medicine. Do yourself a favor and take that medicine whenever you can.

---
# Words to the Wise
---

What about fun? The God who
made giraffes, a baby's
fingernails, a puppy's tail,
a crooknecked squash,
the bobwhite's call, and
a young girl's giggle,
has a sense of humor.
Make no mistake about that.
Catherine Marshall

**Laughter is God's Medicine.**
Henry Ward Beecher

---

# God's Word

---

There is a time for everything,
and everything on earth has its
special season. There is a time
to cry and a time to laugh. There
is a time to be sad and
a time to dance.

Ecclesiastes 3:1,4 NCV

# A Prayer

Dear Lord, laughter is Your gift to me; help me to enjoy it. Today and every day, put a smile on my face, and help me to me share that smile with other people, starting with my family. This is the day that You have made, Lord. Let me enjoy it . . . and let me laugh.

—Amen—

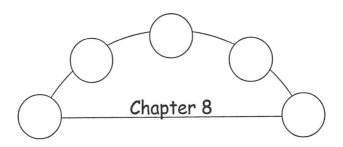

# WHY ARE INNOCENT PEOPLE HURT?

Then Moses returned to the Lord
and said, "Lord, why have you
brought this trouble
on your people?"
—
Exodus 5:22 NCV

Even a good man like Moses couldn't always understand the mysteries of God's plans. And neither can we. Sometimes, people who do nothing wrong get sick; sometimes, innocent people are hurt; sometimes, bad things happen to very good people. And just like Moses, we can't always understand why.

God doesn't explain Himself to us with the clarity that we humans would prefer (think about this: if God *did* explain Himself with perfect clarity, we wouldn't have enough brainpower to understand the explanation that He gave!).

When innocent people are hurt, we question God because we can't figure out exactly what He's doing, or why. Why are innocent people allowed to feel pain and good people allowed to die? Since we can't fully answer that question now, we must trust in God's love, God's wisdom, and God's plan.

And while we're waiting for that wonderful day when all our questions will be answered (in heaven), we should use the time that we have here on earth to help the people who need it most. After all, we will have an eternity to have all our questions answered when we get to heaven. But when it comes to helping other people, we don't have nearly that much time. So let's get busy helping them . . . *right now*!

OUR LIVES ARE IN THE HANDS OF GOD, AND HE IS AIMING AT SOMETHING WE CANNOT SEE.

Oswald Chambers

# Words to the Wise

Pain is not a sign of God's displeasure; it is simply a part of the fiber of our lives.

Fanny Crosby

Our valleys may be filled with foes and tears, but we can lift our eyes to the hills to see God and the angels.

Billy Graham

God's love and His grace is sufficient for all our needs, for every problem and for every difficulty, for every broken heart, and for every human sorrow.

Peter Marshall

THOUGH
OUR FEELINGS
COME AND GO,
GOD'S LOVE
FOR US DOES NOT.

C. S. Lewis

## God's Word

You will be sad, but your sadness
will become joy.
John 16:20 NCV

# A Prayer

Dear Lord, when I have questions
that I can't answer, I will trust
You. And I will do my best to
offer help to those who need it,
so that through me, others,
too, might come to know
You *and* trust You.
—Amen—

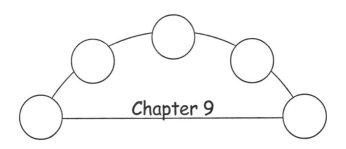

# WHY MUST WE SACRIFICE?

Jesus sat down and called the twelve apostles to him. He said, "Whoever wants to be the most important must be last of all and servant of all."

—

Mark 9:35 NCV

Jesus instructed His disciples to help each other. Those instructions still apply. If we are to be obedient servants of Christ, we must be willing to help those who can't help themselves. In other words, we must become "servants to all."

Some people choose careers that allow them to serve and protect our homes and our world (this includes police officers, firefighters, and those who serve in our military). These brave men and women make *very big sacrifices*, and we should thank them whenever we can.

We, too, can help other people, starting with our families and friends. We can help them with good deeds and with sincere prayers. And that exactly what God wants us to do.

Is someone in your family making a big sacrifice by serving in a dangerous profession? If so, remember that the most important people in God's kingdom are those who serve others.

So let's all offer prayers of thanks for those brave men and women who serve and protect us . . . and let's all do our best to serve *wherever* and *however* we can.

HAVE YOUR TOOLS READY;
GOD WILL FIND YOU
WORK.

Charles Kingsley

# Words to the Wise

If God sends us on stony paths,
He provides strong shoes.
Corrie ten Boom

Pray as if it's all up to God;
behave as if it's all up to you.
Anonymous

HANDS ARE MADE FOR WORK, AND THE HEART IS MADE FOR GOD.

Josepha Rossello

## God's Word

When you do things, do not let
selfishness or pride be your guide.
Be humble and give more honor
to others than to yourselves.

Philippians 2:3 ICB

# A Prayer

Dear Lord, let me help others
in every way that I can. Jesus
served others; I can too. I will
serve other people with my good
deeds and with my prayers, and
I will give thanks for all those
who serve and protect
our nation and our world.
—Amen—

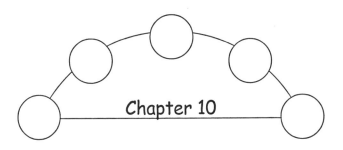

Chapter 10

# MAKING THE WORLD A BETTER PLACE

—

You are the light that gives light to the world. In the same way, you should be a light for other people. Live so that they will see the good things you do and will praise your Father in heaven.

—

Matthew 5:14, 16 NCV

Would you like to make the world a better place? If so, you can start by practicing the Golden Rule.

Some rules are easier to understand than they are to live by, and the Golden Rule certainly fits that description. Jesus told us that we should treat other people in the same way that we would want to be treated (that is the Golden Rule). But sometimes, especially when we're tired or upset, that rule is very hard to follow.

Jesus wants us to treat other people with respect, kindness, love, and courtesy. When we do, we make our families and friends happy . . . and we make our Father in heaven very proud.

So if you're wondering how to make the world a better place, here's a great place to start: let the Golden Rule by *your* rule, too. And if you want to know how to treat other people, ask the person you see every time you look into the mirror. The answer you receive will tell you exactly what to do.

THE GOLDEN RULE STARTS AT HOME, BUT IT SHOULD NEVER STOP THERE.

Marie T. Freeman

# Words to the Wise

Make it a rule, and pray to God
to help you to keep it, never,
if possible, to lie down at night
without being able to say: "I have
made one human being at least
a little wiser, or a little happier,
or at least a little better
this day."
Charles Kingsley

Do all the good you can. By all
the means you can. In all the ways
you can. In all the places you can.
At all the times you can. To all
the people you can. As long
as ever you can.
John Wesley

IF WE HAVE THE TRUE LOVE OF GOD IN OUR HEARTS, WE WILL SHOW IT IN THE WAY THAT WE LIVE OUR LIVES.

D. L. Moody

ONE OF THE NICEST THINGS WE CAN DO FOR OUR HEAVENLY FATHER IS TO BE KIND TO ONE OF HIS CHILDREN.

St. Teresa of Avila

# God's Word

Do to others what you want them
to do to you.
Matthew 7:12 NCV

# A Prayer

Dear Lord, help me always to do
my very best to treat others
as I wish to be treated.
The Golden Rule is Your rule,
Father; let me also make it mine.
—Amen—

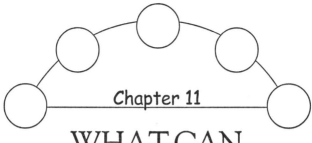

# Chapter 11

# WHAT CAN I DO TO HELP?

Then a Samaritan traveling down the road came to where the hurt man was. When he saw the man, he felt very sorry for him. The Samaritan went to him, poured olive oil and wine on his wounds, and bandaged them. Then he put the hurt man on his own donkey and took him to an inn where he cared for him.

—

Luke 10:33-34 NCV

Sometimes we would like to help make the world a better place, but we're not sure how to do it. Jesus told the story of the "Good Samaritan," a man who helped a fellow traveler when no one else would. We, too, should be good Samaritans when we find people who need our help.

A good place to start helping other people is at home. And of course, we should also offer our help at school and at church.

Another way that we can help other people is to pray for them. God always hears our prayers, so we should talk with Him as often as we can. When we do, we're not only doing a wonderful thing for the people we pray for, we're also doing a wonderful thing for ourselves, too.

When bad things happen in our world, there's always *something* we can do. So what can *you* do to make God's world a better place? You can start by making your own corner of the world a little nicer place to live (by sharing kind words and good deeds). And then, you can take your concerns to God in prayer. Whether you've offered a helping hand or a heartfelt prayer, you've done a lot.

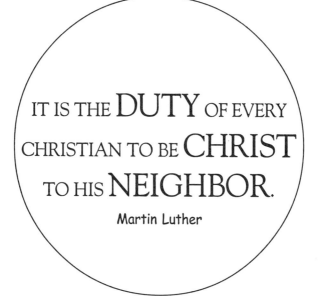

IT IS THE DUTY OF EVERY CHRISTIAN TO BE CHRIST TO HIS NEIGHBOR.

Martin Luther

## Words to the Wise

When you ask God to do
something, don't ask timidly;
put your whole heart into it.
Marie T. Freeman

When you pray for anyone,
you help that person
and you help yourself.
Norman Vincent Peale

GOD IS ALWAYS LISTENING.

Stormie Omartian

# God's Word

Be patient when trouble comes.
Pray at all times.
Romans 12:12 ICB

# A Prayer

Dear Lord, help me to make
Your world a better place. I can't
fix all the world's troubles, but
I *can* help make things better
with kind words, good deeds, and
sincere prayers. Let my actions
and my prayers be pleasing to You,
Lord, now and forever.
—Amen—

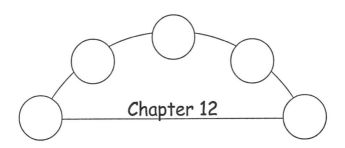

Chapter 12

# HOW CAN
# I FORGIVE?

Be kind and loving to each other,
and forgive each other just as
God forgave you in Christ.

—

Ephesians 4:32 NCV

When people behave badly, it's hard to forgive them, but that's exactly what God tells us to do.

How hard is it to forgive? Sometimes, it's very hard! But God tells us that we must forgive other people, even when we'd rather not. So, if you're angry with anybody (or if you're upset by something you *yourself* have done) it's time to forgive. Right now!

But what if you have already tried to forgive somebody yet simply can't do it? Then you must keep trying.

God instructs you to treat other people exactly as you wish to be treated. And since *you* want to be forgiven for the mistakes that *you* make, you must be willing to extend forgiveness to other people for the mistakes that *they* have made. If you can't seem to forgive someone, you should keep asking God to help you until you do. And you can be sure of this: if you keep asking for God's help, He will give it.

## Words to the Wise

If you can't seem to forgive someone, pray for that person and keep praying for him or her until, with God's help, you've removed the bitterness from your heart.
Marie T. Freeman

Forgiveness is rarely easy, but it is always right.
Cynthia Heald

SOMETIMES,
WE NEED
A HOUSECLEANING
OF THE HEART.

Catherine Marshall

FORGIVENESS
IS GOD'S COMMAND.

Martin Luther

GOD FORGETS THE PAST.
IMITATE HIM.

Max Lucado

FORGIVENESS

IS NOT AN EMOTION

THAT WE FEEL;

IT IS SOMETHING THAT

WE DO.

Corrie ten Boom

## God's Word

Those who show mercy to others are happy, because God will show mercy to them.
Matthew 5:7 NCV

# A Prayer

Dear Lord, sometimes it's very hard to forgive those who have hurt me, but with Your help, I can forgive them. Help me to bring forgiveness into my heart, so that I can forgive others just as You have already forgiven me.
—Amen—

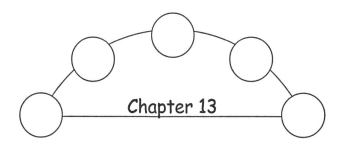

Chapter 13

# GOD IS GOOD, THE LAST WORD IS HIS

I have told you these things so
that you can have peace in me.
In this world you will have trouble.
But be brave! I have overcome
the world!

—

John 16:33 ICB

God is good, and God is in charge—even when bad things happen.

Sometimes, of course, we don't know why things happen as they do. But God does. Yet, the knowledge that God knows exactly what *He* is doing may offer *us* very little comfort. Often, we become discouraged, or worse. When loved ones are taken from us, we cry bitter tears. When we witness the pain of people here at home or the pain of people far away, we wonder why. Sometimes, despite our prayers and our tears, our questions must go unanswered—for now.

Thankfully, there will come a day when our sadness will vanish and our questions will be answered. But until then, we will, on occasion, weep tears of sadness when bad things happen. Why? Because we simply can't understand all the reasons that our world unfolds as it does. Yet God understands, and He has the final word.

God doesn't *answer* all of our questions, but He *does* expect us to do something about them. When we wonder why the world isn't a better place, God expects us to answer that question with willing hands and heartfelt prayers.

As long as God gives us strength, He expects us to continue to work for a better world. Even during life's darkest days, we must continue to love, continue to serve, and continue to protect our neighbors. We must be confident in God's promises *and* in the final victory of eternal life that is ours through the person of God's Son, Jesus Christ.

When we accept God's love and His Son, we receive the Answer (with a capital A) to the troubles of our world. It's precisely that Answer that gives us the hope, the courage, and the faith to trust our Heavenly Father today, tomorrow, and forever.

AS BIG AS THIS
UNIVERSE IS, GOD
HAS COMPLETE POWER
OVER IT.

C. H. Spurgeon

# Words to the Wise

Jesus Christ is the first and last,
author and finisher, the beginning
and end. He must come first.
God never comes next!

Vance Havner

Put your hand into the hand of
God. He gives the calmness
and serenity of heart and soul.

Mrs. Charles E. Cowman

God never leads us astray.
He knows exactly where He's
taking us. Our job is to obey.

Charles Swindoll

GOD TREATS US AS HIS CHILDREN. BECAUSE WE ARE HIS, WE MUST TRUST HIM.

Hannah Whitall Smith

THE GREATEST
LOVE OF ALL IS
GOD'S LOVE FOR US.

Billy Graham

## God's Word

The Lord is my shepherd;
I have everything I need.
Surely your goodness and love will
be with me all my life,
and I will live in the house
of the Lord forever.

Psalm 23:1,6 NCV

## A Prayer

Dear Lord, I will turn my
concerns over to You. I will
trust Your love, Your Wisdom,
Your plan, Your Promises,
and Your Son—today
and every day that I live.
—Amen—

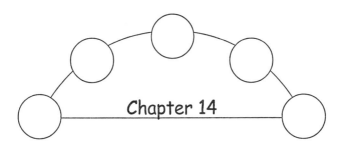

Chapter 14

# QUESTIONS AND ANSWERS FOR KIDS

After three days they found Jesus sitting in the Temple with the teachers, listening to them and asking them questions. All who heard him were amazed at his understanding and answers.
—

Luke 2:46-47 NCV

# QUESTION

Why does God allow
bad things to happen?

# ANSWER

We don't fully understand why
bad things happen. Sometimes, of
course, people disobey God's laws
and invite troubles and heartbreak
into our world. But other times, bad
things happen, and we don't know
why. Yet even when we can't understand why things happen, we can still
trust that God is our loving Father.
And we can trust that despite our
pain, God can still create good things
out of bad circumstances.

# Q̶UESTION

Why do people have to die?

# A̶NSWER

Life and death is a part of God's plan: in the Book of Ecclesiastes, we read that there is "a time to be born and a time to die" (3:2 NCV). God sent His Son Jesus to offer us eternal life. That gift is a priceless possession, an expression of God's perfect love for us. That's why we must accept God's plan for our lives by inviting His Son into our hearts.

# (Q)UESTION

If Bible Says We Should Love
Our Enemies,
Why Must We Fight Them?

# (A)NSWER

The Bible recognizes that evil exists in our world. Good people must not ignore evil; they must, instead, fight for justice and freedom. Even Jesus, when confronting moneychangers in the Temple, reacted forcefully; so, too, must those who serve and protect us.

# (Q)UESTION

What can I do for hurting people
around the world?

# (A)NSWER

There's a lot you can do. First,
you can pray for people around the
world (and you can be sure that God
will hear your prayers). Then, you
can ask your parents or grandparents to help you think of other
things that you can do to help. And
don't forget your church: very
often, your church will organize
ways to extend a helping hand to
people around the world, and when
your church gets involved, you
should help.

# QUESTION

### If I'm afraid, whom should I talk to?

# ANSWER

If you're afraid, for any reason, tell a grownup, starting, of course, with the grownups who love and care for you.

# (Q)UESTION

What if I can't sleep?

# (A)NSWER

If you're having trouble sleeping,
try these tips:

1. Stop drinking drinks that contain caffeine (ask your parents to help you select drinks that won't keep you awake);

2. Don't watch TV shows right before going to bed (they can make you too nervous, too excited, or too worried to get a good night's sleep);

3. If you can't sleep at night, don't take long naps during the day (especially naps in the late afternoon);

4. Go to sleep at the same time every night (it helps to establish regular sleeping habits).

# (Q)UESTION

What if I have bad dreams?

# (A)NSWER

Remember this: everybody has bad dreams occasionally, and so will you. But if you're having *lots* of bad dreams, it may be time to look at the things you're putting *into* your brain while you're awake! Here are a few things to try:

1. Cut back on the amount of television that you watch (especially in the evenings);

2. Spend more time *talking* about your worries (especially by talking to the grownups in your life) and less time *worrying* about your worries; and if you have concerns that you haven't yet talked about, don't keep them all bottled up inside; talk about them;

3. Every night before you go to bed, be sure that you've spent plenty of time praying to God and thanking Him for His blessings;

4. And if you keep having lots of bad dreams, tell your parents or grandparents; they can help!

# QUESTION

When I'm sad, is it okay to cry?

# ANSWER

Of course it's okay to cry (yes, even Jesus cried). In fact, sometimes, a "good cry" will make you feel better. So if you're sad and you feel like crying, remember that if it was okay for Jesus, it's okay for the rest of us, too.

# (Q)UESTION

I'm sad all of the time,
what should I do?

# (A)NSWER

If you feel sad some of the time, welcome to the club. But if you're feeling sad *most of the time*, you should tell your parents (or grandparents) how you feel. If you don't tell them, they may have trouble figuring out your feelings, and that makes it harder for them to help you.

# $\widehat{Q}$UESTION

Forgiveness is hard.
How can I "forgive and forget?"

# $\widehat{A}$NSWER

Even when we can't "forget," we can "forgive"—eventually. Sometimes, of course, it's takes a long time to forgive other people, but if we keep trying to forgive—and if we keep asking God to help us forgive— we will eventually discover the peace that forgiveness can bring to our hearts.

# (Q)UESTION

What if a family member
or friend is serving in
a dangerous occupation?

# (A)NSWER

If so, you'll be worried from time
to time. You should talk about your
worries with grownups who love you,
and you should also pray about your
concerns to your Father in Heaven.

# (Q)UESTION

If I'm hurting now,
will the pain always be this bad?

# (A)NSWER

If you're worried or sad, you may believe that you'll feel this way forever. But you can be sure that you'll feel better in time. God uses time to help heal our wounds, and He will use time to heal your wounds, too.

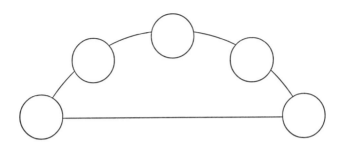

# BIBLE VERSES
# TO REMEMBER

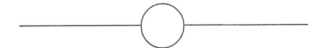

If you love me,
you will obey my commands.
—

Psalm 86:15 NCV

# The Promise of Eternal Life

I TELL YOU THE TRUTH, WHOEVER BELIEVES HAS ETERNAL LIFE.

John 6:47 NCV

# Jesus is the Way

JESUS ANSWERED,
"I AM THE WAY,
AND THE TRUTH,
AND THE LIFE.
THE ONLY WAY TO THE FATHER
IS THROUGH ME."

John 14:6 NCV

# Serve God with a Smile

SERVE THE LORD WITH JOY; COME BEFORE HIM WITH SINGING.

Psalm 100:2 NCV

# Be Happy Every Day

THIS IS THE DAY
THAT THE LORD HAS MADE.
LET US REJOICE
AND BE GLAD TODAY!

Psalm 118:24 NCV

# God Gives Hope

CRYING MAY LAST FOR A NIGHT, BUT JOY COMES IN THE MORNING.

Psalm 30:5 NCV

# Have Faith in God

JESUS SAID,
"DON'T LET YOUR HEARTS
BE TROUBLED.
TRUST IN GOD,
AND TRUST IN ME."

**John 14:1 ICB**

# God Gives Us Inner Strength

I CAN DO ALL THINGS THROUGH CHRIST, BECAUSE HE GIVES ME STRENGTH.

Philippians 4:13 NCV

# God's Word Is the Truth

THEN YOU WILL KNOW THE TRUTH, AND THE TRUTH WILL MAKE YOU FREE.

John 8:32 NCV

# God Works Miracles

## GOD CAN DO ANYTHING!

Luke 1:37 NCV

# Love All People

LOVE EACH OTHER DEEPLY WITH ALL YOUR HEART.

1 Peter 1:22 NCV

# God Will Take Away Your Worries

SO DON'T WORRY
ABOUT TOMORROW.
EACH DAY HAS ENOUGH
TROUBLE OF ITS OWN.
TOMORROW WILL
HAVE ITS OWN WORRIES.

Matthew 6:34 ICB

# The Golden Rule

DO TO OTHERS
WHAT YOU WANT
THEM TO DO TO YOU.

Matthew 7:12 NCV

# God's Gift to Us

GOD LOVED
THE WORLD SO MUCH
THAT HE GAVE HIS ONE
AND ONLY SON SO THAT
WHOEVER BELIEVES IN
HIM MAY NOT BE LOST, BUT
HAVE ETERNAL LIFE.

John 3:16 ncv

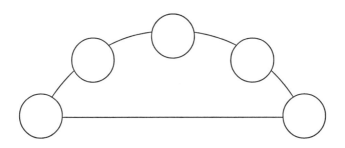

# A FEW TIPS
# FOR PARENTS

Trust the Lord with all your heart,
and don't depend on
your own understanding.
Proverbs 3:5 NCV

### Supervise
### What They Watch . . .
### *Very* Carefully:

Your home needs a strict media censor: you! Television contains far too many disturbing images for children (and, for that matter, for adults, too). Unsupervised television usually spells trouble for kids; don't let it spell trouble for *your* kids.

## Remember:
## You Set the Emotional Tone:

If you're disturbed by your child's reaction to the troubling events of the world, perhaps it's time to take stock of your own reactions. Remember that as an adult, you'll set the emotional tone for your family; be certain that your own response to our world's troubling events is the same kind of reaction that you want your children to have (because it will be).

## Make Your Home a Place Where Your Child Can Feel Safe:

Even though the world is a dangerous place, you must assure your child that he or she can feel protected and safe *with you*. As your child's protector, you have done your best to create a safe, supportive environment. Remind your child that his or her safety is your responsibility and your concern—and that you're up to the task.

## Watch for Changes in Behavior or Attitude:

Nobody knows your child like you do. Watch for changes in behavior, demeanor, eating habits, and sleeping patterns. And if you observe changes in your child's behavior that give you cause for genuine concern, seek the advice of your doctor, your pastor, or a trained mental health professional.

## Talk About It:

In our information-saturated society, we simply can't protect our children from all the harsh realities of our troubled world. Thus, we must talk with our children about these events in ways that are appropriate to our youngsters' current levels of understanding. Should our kids see every image and know every detail about the world's strife and suffering? Of course not. But it's inevitable that children will see disturbing images, so you need to be ready and willing to talk with your child about the questions and concerns that will surely arise.

## You Don't Have to Know Everything:

If you don't have all the answers, that's okay. Sometimes, it's perfectly acceptable to say "I don't know," *even* if you're a parent.

## It's Okay to Be Sad:

Remind you child that when bad things happen, it's okay to be sad, and it's okay to cry. And don't be ashamed of your own tears, either.

## Be Aware of the Difference Between Sadness and Depression:

The sadness that accompanies any significant loss is an inevitable fact of life. In time, sadness runs its course and gradually abates. Depression, on the other hand, is a physical and emotional condition that is, in almost all cases, treatable with medication and counseling. Depression is not a disease to be taken lightly. If you notice changes in yourself or your child that cause concern, consult your doctor or a mental health professional immediately.

## If You're Worried, Ask for Help:

If you have reason to suspect that your child is in significant emotional distress, seek the help of a trained professional. Doctors, counselors, and pastors are trained to help you determine whether or not additional assistance is needed for your child. If you have reason to be concerned about your child's welfare, don't hesitate to seek help.